THE REALITY OF REALITY TV WORKBOOK

A Publication by On the Lot Productions, LLC
New Orleans, La

On the Lot the Lot Productions, LLC
Publisher since 2005
www.onthelotproductions.com

™ is registered trademarks of On the Lot Productions, LLC (Logo created by Melanie Bledsoe)

Copyright ©2011 by Dr. Melissa C Caudle
All rights reserved

Distributed by Create Space Amazon.com

ISBN – 978-1460921593

Cover Designed by Dr. Melissa Caudle

Graphic Logos for all reality shows in this book created by Dr. Melissa Caudle and are Copyright Protected

Cover Photo by Salvatore Vuono
Author Picture by Robert Zaning of Zaning Portrait Studios
Introduction Photo by Salvatore Vuono
Chapter 1 photo by Bulldogza
Chapter 2 photo by Dr. Melissa Caudle
Chapter 3 photo by Salvatore Vuono
Chapter 4 photo by Salvatore Vuono
Chapter 5 photo by Salvatore Vuono
Chapter 6 photo by Graur Razvan Ionut
Chapter 7 photo by Salvatore Vuono
Chapter 8 photo by Salvatore Vuono
Chapter 9 photo by Salvatore Vuono
Chapter 10 photo by Carlos Porto
Chapter 11 photo by Renjith Krishnan
Chapter 12 photo by Renjith Krishnan
Chapter 13 photo by Renjith Krishnan
Chapter 14 photo by Pixomar
Chapter 15 photo by Dr. Melissa Caudle
Chapter 16 photo by Pixomar
Chapter 17 photo by Simon Howden and Graphic Page Dr. Melissa Caudle
Chapter 18 photo by Simon Howden
Chapter 19 photo and business plan cover created by Dr. Melissa Caudle
All other photos taken by Dr. Melissa Caudle

All photos in the book have been used with the permission of their copyright owners and/or www.freedigitalphotos.net

Printed in the United States of America

THE REALITY OF REALITY TV

WORKBOOK

Dr. Melissa Caudle

COPPYRIGHT 2011 ©   Dr. Melissa Caudle
ALL RIGHTS RESERVED

This book is copyright protected and registered with the United States Library of Congress. No part may be used in any capacity, dupicated or replicated without the consent of the author. If you want to use any portion of the contents in a magazine article, newspaper, or your webiste, please contact the author at drmelcaudle@aol.com for written permission.

TABLE OF CONTENTS

Introduction 1
Chapter 1: The Big Idea 5
    Worksheet 1 - Reality Show Genres 6
    Worksheet 2 - Concept Development 7
    Worksheet 3 - The Five Big "Ws" 8
Chapter 2: The Reality of Show Business 9
    Worksheet 4 - Title of Your Show 10
    Worksheet 5 - Graphics 11
Chapter 3: Confidentiality 13
    Confidentiality Log 14
Chapter 4: The Executive Summary 15
    Worksheet 6 – Opening Statement 16
    Worksheet 7 – Project Overview 17
    Worksheet 8 – Trend Statement 18
    Worksheet 9 – Cast Members 19
    Worksheet 10 – Production Team 20
    Worksheet 11 - Product-Placement 21
    Worksheet 12- Distribution and Marketing 22
    Worksheet 13 - Investment Opportunity 23
Chapter 5: Logline and Synopsis 25
    Worksheet 14 - Logline 27
Chapter 6: The Reality Show Format 29
    Worksheet 16 - Format and Structure 30
Chapter 7: Cast 33
    Worksheet 17 – Your Cast 34
    Worksheet 18 - Cast Information 35
    Worksheet 19 - Cast Bios 36
Chapter 8: The Production Team 39
    Worksheet 20 – The Company 40
    Worksheet 21- Producer 41
    Worksheet 22 – Director 42
    Worksheet 23 – Consultants and Affiliates 43
Chapter 9: Production 45
    Worksheet 24- Production Section 46
Chapter 10: Reality Show Statistics 47
    Worksheet 25 - Market Trend 48
    Worksheet 26 - Industry Trend 49
Chapter 11: Product-Placement 51
    Worksheet 27 - Product-Placement Items 52
    Worksheet 28 – Product-Placement Table 54
Chapter 12: Distribution 55
    Worksheet 29- Press Releases 56

Chapter 13 Marketing Strategies 59
    Worksheet 30 - Marketing Strategies 60
    Worksheet 31 - Marketing Statement 61
Chapter 14: Investment Opportunity 63
  (No Worksheet; information goes directly into plan from companion book)
Chapter 15: The One Pager 65
    Worksheet 32 - Developing Your One Pager 66
Chapter 16: The Budget 69
    Worksheet 33 - Line Items 70
    Worksheet 34 - Potential Crew 72
    Worksheet 35 - Potential Vendors 73
    Worksheet 36 - Potential Locations 74
    Worksheet 37 - Budget Projection 75
Chapter 17: Putting it All Together 77
    Worksheet 38 – Editing and Formatting 78
    Worksheet 39 - Checklist for Business Plan 79
Chapter 18: First Contact 81
    Worksheet 40 - Network Contacts 82
    Worksheet 41 - The Agent Query Letter 84
    Worksheet 42 - The Network Query Letter 85
    Worksheet 43 - Prodution Query Letter 86
Chapter 19: Going Forward 87
About the Author 89
Index 93

Note: This book is the companion Workbook to the book ***The Reality of Reality TV: Reality Show Business Plans*** written by Dr. Melissa Caudle. The information may not be useful or make sense if you do not obtain the companion book. If you do not currently own the companion book and wish to do so, you may also purchase it by visiting www.onthelotproductions.com, Amazon.com CreateSpace eStore, CreateSpace Direct, Barnes and Noble and other retail stores. For additional information contact drmelcaudle@gmail.com.

DISCLAIMER

Dr. Melissa Caudle, On the Lot Productions, LLC, nor the publisher cannot gauruntee that by following the information in this book will obtain any source of funding for your project.

This book was written for educational purposes only and not as legal, tax, or accounting advise. We cannot be responsible for any documents that you formulate as a result of this book. We cannot take any responsible with what the reader does with the informaiton we provide and any documents the reader produces should be reviewed by a qualified entertainment attorney in the state in which you live. Each state has unique laws.

Likewise, only an attorney can give legal advise and only an accountant can give financial advice.

It is recommended by the author that the reader also purchase the companion book to this Workbook called *The Reality of Reality TV: Reality Show Business Plans*. This Workbook is not intended to be purchased and used without it's companion book. If you desire to obtain a copy of *The Reality of Reality TV: Reality Show Business Plans* it is available from Amazon.com, www.onthelotproductions.com, Amazon.com CreateSpace eStore, CreateSpace Direct, Barnes and Noble and other retail stores. For additional information contact drmelcaudle@gmail.com. (ISBN – 978-1460916988) or through www.onthelotproductions.com.

DEDICATION

I dedicate this workbook to all of the focus group members that suggested that I create a separate 8 X 10 Workbook that goes along with my book *The Reality of Reality TV*: Reality *Show Business Plans*. Thank you for your suggestions and the time you spent with me. I can't wait to watch one of your reality shows someday as a result of your participation.

SPECIAL THANKS

There are many people that I need to thank in their support and encouragement. I'm really afraid that I will miss someone and hurt their feelings. Believe me that is not my intent. So I'll apologize now to anyone that I may not personally mention.

The first thank you has to go to my Mom, Helen Ray, and to my Dad, William Ray, without question for making me believe that I could be anything I wanted to be just as long I was the best at it. Without them none of this would have been possible.

Next I want to express my gratitude to my mentors and to all that have challenged me who include Line Producer Beau Marks and Director/Screenwriter Steve Esteb. All have a special place in my heart for helping me to develop into the producer that I am today.

The next group includes my peers and those that I have worked with on numerous films and reality shows over the last couple of years. I would be remiss if I didn't mention by name J.P Preito who I met on the reality show *The Girls Next Door* and who I still today value his opinion. Also to all crew members on all reality shows that work so hard behind the scenes. Each of you are so amazing and talented and set an example others should follow. Lastly, I commend each independent producer and director out there that follow their dreams.

Then I want to thank my family who has always supported me no matter what. To my siblings, Denny, Caylen and Robby who always encourage me to be my best and to write and be creative. Especially Robby, my sister, who placed the initial challenge and idea for me to write this book as she did with my very first one. Next are my three daughters and their families. Without exception they are my best-friends and allow me to be who I am today. Each daughter reflects a different part me. Erin represents my educator and writer side and keeps me grounded to help others as she is a third grade teacher. Kelly represents my business side always guiding me in business and marketing matters as she is a business woman. My youngest, Jamie, represents my creative side in the television and film industry as she is an actress in Los Angeles.

Last but not least, to my husband and my best-friend, Mike, who always allows me the space and time to fulfill my dream.

INTRODUCTION

HOW TO USE THIS BOOK

Stop! Don't read this book or complete the worksheets without first buying my companion book *The Reality of Reality TV: Reality Show Business Plans* available on Amazon.com, CreateSpace eStore, CreateSpace Direct, Barnes and Noble and other retail outlets (ISBN – 978-1460916988). Otherwise the contents of this workbook won't make much sense. You have to trust me on this. The book and the workbook are meant to go together like peanut butter and jelly or milk and chocolate chip cookies. Just like *Lays* potato chips you can't just have one. Therefore, if you haven't already purchased the companion book do not waste any time and go directly to Amazon.com, Barnes and Noble, Create eStore or other retail outlets and buy it today without reservation or hesitation. **IT IS A MUST.**

Then when your copy arrives jump in and start your journey. Read it one chapter at a time and absorb the contents. After you read each chapter apply what you learn immediately while writing each section tailored to your show by using the worksheets in this book. This is how I intended for you to get the most out of your experience. It's that important.

This workbook provides worksheets and forms directly from the companion book *The Reality of Reality TV: Reality Show Business Plans*. In each chapter of the companion book I explain each section of a reality show business plan. I guide you through the process of writing that section, provide examples from actual reality show business plans and then provide you with practical applications so that you put what you just learned into creative action. It is during the practical application stage that I get you to develop your plan one step at a time using these worksheets. I urge you to complete the practical applications and keep them in a notebook binder. And, **DO NOT** discard them. You will refer to them often in your journey to complete your reality show business plan.

WHY YOU SHOULD BUY THIS BOOK

You should buy this book because it is the perfect companion to *The Reality of Reality TV: Reality Show Business Plans* and is written in layman's terms. There is nothing else that can compare to this workbook or the companion book *The Reality of Reality TV: Reality Show Business Plans.* It is easy to follow and the worksheets provide you a step-by-step format to assist in developing your reality show business plan. However, I wouldn't buy this workbook just by itself without the companion book. I personally don't think you can accomplish the task of creating a reality show business plan by simply utilizing these worksheets alone. You need the information from the companion book for it all to make sense. You goal is to create an effective reality show business plan that you can take to network television executives, isn't it? Then don't fool yourself by trying to take a shortcut and only buying one or the other of my books. You need both. However, if you can only afford one of them, I suggest you get the companion book *The Reality of Reality TV: Reality Show Business Plans* and forgo the purchase of the workbook. Why? Because the worksheets in this book are also in the companion book but are smaller in size. I designed this workbook after several focus groups asked me to do so. They wanted it so I wrote it. It's the supply and demand business philosophy in action.

ITEMS THAT GO WITH THIS BOOK

After the three focus groups met to discuss this book one of the biggest feedbacks I received was they wish there was a Word Template available for the reality show business plan as well as a training tape. I listened and responded to their suggestions and feedback. Other products by Dr. Mel Caudle include:

The Reality of Reality TV: Reality Show Business Plans is a 410 page step-by-step guided approach to writing business plans for reality shows. This is must have book for all reality show creators and producers. This book is available at Amazon.com, www.onthelotproductions.com, Amazon.com CreateSpace eStore, CreateSpace Direct, Barnes and Noble and other retail stores. For additional information contact drmelcaudle@gmail.com. (ISBN – 978-1460916988) or through www.onthelotproductions.com.

The Reality of Reality TV Word Template is a Microsoft Word template is available for purchase. I recommend that you purchase this template when writing your reality show business plan. There is no need to reinvent the wheel and it will save you hours of time in formatting your reality show business plan or pitch packet. The template that accompanies this book is available by emailing me or contacting me through my website at www.onthelotproductions.com. When you contact me be sure to put the following code in your subject matter: RTV-327. That way I can get you the right template.

The Reality of Reality TV DVD Series is in the works. This will be a series of videos where I teach you the process of writing reality show business plans. All topics covered in this book will be addressed as well as conversations with me with other reality show creators and producers. Stay tuned as this series develops. Check my production website often for its availability. This series will also be made available from Amazon.com, www.onthelotproductions.com, Amazon.com CreateSpace eStore, CreateSpace Direct, Barnes and Noble and other retail stores. For additional information contact drmelcaudle@gmail.com. or through www.onthelotproductions.com.

150 Ways to Fund a Reality Show, by Dr. Melissa Caudle, is a book that provides ways to raise money to produce a reality show. These methods have been used by the author and shared with others. Also in the book are additional marketing strategies. This book will be made available from Amazon.com, www.onthelotproductions.com, Amazon.com CreateSpace eStore, CreateSpace Direct, Barnes and Noble and other retail stores. For additional information contact drmelcaudle@gmail.com. or through www.onthelotproductions.com. (ISBN 13- 978-460967133 or ISBN 10- 146096715).

PHOTO CREDIT FOR INTRODUCTION

Hand and Stop Button by Indiego/freedigitalphoto.net

Cover Design of *The Reality of Reality TV: Reality Show Business Plans* created by Dr. Melissa Caudle and film photo taken by Salvatore Vuono.

Risk = Reward graphic designed by On the Lot Productions, LLC

NOTES

CHAPTER 1 WORKSHEETS
THE BIG IDEA

Photo by Bulldogs

WORKSHEET 1: REALITY SHOW GENRES

Objective: To identify types of reality show genres.
Review Table 1 and add reality shows currently on television to the appropriate genre.

Documentary	Game Show
Temptation Island	Who Wants to Be a Millionaire
Life Drama	**Dating Shows**
The Secret Millionaire	The Bachelor
Special Environment	**Celebrity**
Temptation Island	Dancing with the Stars
Competition	**Surveillance**
American Idol	Big Brother
Talk Shows	**Professional Activities**
The Oprah Winfrey Show	Miami Ink

WORKSHEET 2: CONCEPT DEVELOPMENT

Objective: To identify working concept of your reality show.

Reality Show Project Working Title:_____

REALITY GENRE *(Check the genre that best identifies your reality show)*

- ☐ Documentary   ☐ Game Show   ☐ Life Drama
- ☐ Celebrity   ☐ Professional   ☐ Paranormal
- ☐ Dating Show   ☐ Makeover   ☐ Competition
- ☐ Talk Show

POTENTIAL CAST *(Check the DESCRIPTION that best identifies your CAST)*

- ☐ ONE CELEBRITY   ☐ INDIVIDUAL   ☐ TWO MAIN CHARACTORS
- ☐ MULTI-CELEBRITIES   ☐ MULTI-GROUP   ☐ MORE THAN TEN PEOPLE

LOCATION *(Check the DESCRIPTION that best identifies your CAST)*

- ☐ House   ☐ Business   ☐ Studio   ☐ Wilderness   ☐ Other

Describe: _____

PROJECT IMPORTANCE

- ☐ Tells a story   ☐ Teaches Something   ☐ Social Issue
- ☐ Entertaining   ☐ Someone Wins   ☐ To Change a Life
- ☐ Political   ☐ To Hook up People   ☐ Makes a Realebrity

WORKSHEET 3: THE BIG 5 Ws

Objective: To identify the Big 5 "W's" for your reality show.

Every good reality show starts with a great concept which includes the Big 5 Ws, which includes who, what, when, where, and why.

To help generate your own reality show concept, complete the following brainstorming exercise.

If you are producing the show yourself generate as many ideas as you can. If you have producing partners, each should complete the exercise and then discuss it and finalize one worksheet that combines the group ideas.

Who is this reality show about?
_____
_____
_____

What will the show be about?
_____
_____
_____
_____

When will the show take place?
_____
_____
_____
_____

Where will the show take place?
_____
_____

Why is this show of interest to others?
_____
_____
_____
_____

CHAPTER 2 WORKSHEETS

THE REALITY SHOW BUSINESS PLAN

Graphics by Dr. Mel Caudle Copyright© 2011

WORKSHEET 4: Title Your Show

Objective: To create a title for your reality show.

The name of your reality show is important. Review worksheets 1-3 to refresh what your show is about. Now it is time to brainstorm your reality show's title by completing each section. You will generate a variety of titles ranging from one word to four or more. List as many as you can.

ONE WILL LIKELY BECOME YOUR TITLE.

ONE WORD TITLES	TWO WORD TITLES	THREE PLUS WORD TITLES

From the list above circle your top five choices.

From the top five circled choices narrow your title to two.

1. _____
2. _____

Now choose your title: _____

WORKSHEET 5: GRAPHICS

Objective: To learn the importance of branding with graphics.

The graphics for your reality show is extremely important to have in your business plan. It needs to be simple, colorful and relate what the show is about without anyone needing to read the logline or synopsis.

Review the following graphic for the *Ace Mechanic* reality show and answer the following questions.

What do you think this show is about?

Who do you think it is about?

Where do you think it was filmed; e.g. location?

ANSWER: The show follows an automobile repairman that is the very best at what he does. There is no problem he can't fix. Other mechanics come to him for training and to solve problems they can't. It was filmed in an automobile repair shop located on HWY 603 in Mississippi.

NOTES

CHAPTER 3 WORKSHEETS

CONFIDENTIALITY

Photo by Salvatore Vuono

CONFIDENTIALITY LOG

REALITY SHOW: _____

Name of Recipient	Name of their Company	Date Sent	Method	Confidentiality Form Received back on	Contact Information
Mark Stanford	BET Ent.	9/3/2011	Hand Delivered	Yes 9/2/2011	1589 XXXXXXX Street Los Angeles, CA XXXXX Email: XXXX@betent@yahoo.com

Copyright© 2011 On the Lot Productions, LLC

Note: Use a separate log for each reality show.

CHAPTER 4 WORKSHEETS

THE EXECUTIVE SUMMARY

Photo by Salvatore Vuono

WORKSHEET 6: OPENING STATEMENT

Objective: To create an Opening Statement for the Executive Summary section of your reality show business plan.

Applying the five "Ws" you will create your opening statement following the below format:

> Post Season, LLC is a Louisiana Limited Liability Company seeking $475,000 for the production of *Post Season* an eight (8) episode reality show with each episode consisting of 45 minutes and product placement endorsements. Post Season will be filmed during the Off-Season of the NFL football league in New Orleans, LA and include five (5) current or former New Orleans Saints Champion football team members who are preparing for "life" after the NFL.

1. Fill in the blanks with your information specific to your reality show.

What is the name of my company? _____

How much funding are you seeking? _____

What is the name of your reality show? _____

How many episodes are you planning on filming? _____

How long is each episode? ____ If it is only a pilot indicate: ___Yes

When will you film your show? _____

What city and state will you film your show? _____

Who are your cast members: _____

2. Following the above sample put together your opening statement three different ways. Then choose the one you prefer.

3. Transfer your opening statement into your reality show business document that you have been creating. Print a hardcopy and place in your binder.

WORKSHEET 7: PROJECT OVERVIEW

Objective: Create the Overview Statement for the Executive Summary section for your reality show business plan.

Using the following statement as a template identify your target areas.

> *Darren: Sharper than Ever,* is a 13 episode reality show that combines the love of sports with professional football with a target audience ranging from age 9 to 90. Anyone that loves football and following a professional athlete will love this show.

1. Identify your target age range audience for your show. Why?

2. What type of person is likely to watch your show? Why?

3. What are the attributes for your show? Why?

4. What will viewers find appealing? Why:

5. What about your show is unique and different from any other currently produced show?

6. Look at your answers above. Circle the age of your audience, the type of audience, the key attributes etc.

7. Using the information you circled and formulate two or three opening statements.

8. Choose the best opening statement from step 7 and type it into your reality show business document. Print a hardcopy and put in your binder.

WORKSHEET 8: REALITY TREND STATEMENT

Objective: To create the Marketing Trend Statement for your reality show proposal.

1. Using the format below type in the standard wording provided below into your reality show document. You will not have the figures yet so keep the Xs. At a later time you will replace the Xs after you have conducted your research. This is a work in progress.

> *The market for reality shows grossed **$X** dollars in 2010 in the U.S. and **$X** worldwide respectively. The success of reality shows similar to **(Name of your reality show)** is evident as shows like **XXXXXXXXX** and **XXXXXXXX** continue to air on **XXXX** and **XXXXX** networks. Audience market appeal for this type of programming continues as networks strive to fulfill the demand. **(Name of your reality show)** offers an opportunity to tap into this market and offers the dimension for high returns with low production cost.*

2. Look up the definition to gross and net income to gain an understanding of the terms.

3. Begin researching gross income for 10 reality shows that fit into your genre of reality show programming. How much has each earned? Keep this information handy and in your binder so that when it comes to creating the section in your reality show business plan you will have the information for quick reference.

WORKSHEET 9: CAST MEMBERS

Objective: To identify the cast to be attached to your show.

1. What type of cast do you have for your show? Check all that apply.

    ☐ Attached Celebrity Cast

    ☐ Want Celebrities but don't have them attached

    ☐ Unknown individuals already attached

    ☐ Unknown individuals needs to be attached

2. Generate a list of possible celebrities that could be included. If not as the main cast, but as the possible host of the show.

3. Generate a list of people that you know that would make great cast members.

4. List any and all people that have agreed to be in your show.

5. Generate 2 to 3 sample statements that identifies your type of cast and who is and is not attached by following the samples in Chapter 4 of the companion book *The Reality of Reality TV: Reality Show Business Plans*.

6. Choose the best one and type it into your reality show business document. Print a hardcopy and put in your binder.

WORKSHEET 10 PRODUCTION TEAM

Objective: To generate the Production Team Statement for the Executive Summary.

1. What is the name of your production company?

2. What type of company is it? Check the one that applies.
   ☐ LLC   ☐ Partnership   ☐ Sole Proprietor   ☐ Other

3. List all producers and experience with reality shows.

4. Who is the director of this project? Is the director attached to the show? ☐ Yes   ☐ No

5. What is the director's experience with reality shows?

6. Who is the producer of this project? Is the producer attached to the show? ☐ Yes   ☐ No

7. What is the producer's experience with reality shows?

8. Generate your Executive Summary Statements using this format and then type it into your reality show business plan.

> *(Name of your production company)* production company will be producing *(Name of Show)*. This is the *(state number)* time the production company has produced a reality show. *(Name of Producer)* is the producer for the show and has produced *(state number)* of reality shows. Additionally, *(Name of Director)* will be the Director and has directed *(state number)* of reality shows

WORKSHEET 11: PRODUCT- PLACEMENT

Objective: Use Worksheet 10 to generate product-placement opportunities specifically for your reality show.

1. Generate a list of at least 10 products that can be used by your cast members.

   1. _____   6. _____
   2. _____   7. _____
   3. _____   8. _____
   4. _____   9. _____
   5. _____   10. _____

2. Generate a list a vendors that your company currently does business with.

3. Using the sample format provided in this chapter choose two to three of the products from the above list that hold the most potential to increase advertising dollars.

   Many opportunities for segment/demo-specific are available for (Name of reality show.) They include but are not limited to: XXXXXX, XXXXX, XXXXX and blank. (Name of Company) will actively seek product endorsements to increase market appeal and advertising revenue sources.

4. Formulate your product-placement statement following the format provided in this chapter and type it into your reality show business plan document.

WORKSHEET 12: DISTRIBUTION AND MARKETING

Objective: To generate distribution and marketing strategies.

1. Generate at least 10 distribution strategies.

2. Generate as many marketing strategies that you can identify.

5. Using the format provided in this chapter create your Distribution and Marketing Strategy statement for your Executive Summary by replacing the bold type in your plan.

> The success of reality shows is directly related to the distribution and marketing strategy. **(Name of Company)** will not sit idle and intends to pitch **(Name of reality show)** to the National Association of Television Producers and Executives annual conference as well as appropriate festivals. Likewise **(Name of Company)** will actively seek to negotiate with appropriate distribution companies known to distribute like genre programming the production. Additionally, all best efforts to market **(Name of reality show)** will begin during production that includes: **(list your ways you identified above)** for said reality show and cast members, create an EPK package, and seek publicity in magazines and newspapers. The distribution and marketing strategies are likely to maximize **(Name of Company)** position for future acquisition by networks and distributors as well as increase future profit **(Name of reality show)** may earn.

6. Type your Distribution and Marketing Strategy statement into your reality show business plan. Print a hardcopy and put it into your binder.

WORKSHEET 13: INVESTMENT OPPORTUNITY

Objective: To create the Investment Opportunity Statement format for your reality show business proposal.

1. Although your numbers will be left blank for now, using the sample in Chapter 4, type in the shell of your Investment Opportunity Statement into your reality show business plan by replacing the bold type print below.

> **(Name of Company)** seeks $X to fund the reality show **(Name of reality show)**. **(Name of Company)** desires to obtain all funding from private investors. Investing in any reality is risky and there is no guarantee that there will be a return on investment. **This is a reality show business plan.** It does not imply and shall not be construed as an offering of securities. Prospective investors are not to construe the contents of this document as investment, legal or tax advice from either the Company or the preparers of this document. Any prospective investor should consult with professional investment advisors and gain professional legal and tax advice. Each potential investor specifically understands and agrees that any estimates, projections, revenue models, forecasts or assumptions are by definition uncertain and thus possibly unreliable. Any party considering a transaction with the Company agrees to look solely to its own due diligence. **(Name of Company)** projects gross revenue of approximately $X with a net producer/investor profit of $X for **(Name of Reality Show)**.

2. Continue conducting research on risk statements on the internet.

NOTES

CHAPTER 5 WORKSHEETS

LOGLINE AND SYNOPSIS

Photo by Salvatore Vuono

WORKSHEET 14: LOGLINE

Objective: To create the logline for your reality show.

1. Generate 10 loglines for your reality show by filling in the blanks.

[Subject] [Verb] [Action] [Outcome]

(A group of college basketball players) (engage) (in life of the court) (as they develop team dynamics)

1. _____ _____ _____ _____.
   Subject   Verb   Action   Outcome

2. _____ _____ _____ _____.
   Subject   Verb   Action   Outcome

3. _____ _____ _____ _____.
   Subject   Verb   Action   Outcome

4. _____ _____ _____ _____.
   Subject   Verb   Action   Outcome

5. _____ _____ _____ _____.
   Subject   Verb   Action   Outcome

6. _____ _____ _____ _____.
   Subject   Verb   Action   Outcome

7. _____ _____ _____ _____.
   Subject   Verb   Action   Outcome

8. _____ _____ _____ _____.
   Subject   Verb   Action   Outcome

9. _____ _____ _____ _____.
   Subject   Verb   Action   Outcome

10. _____ _____ _____ _____.
    Subject   Verb   Action   Outcome

LOGLINE AND SYNOPSIS

WORKSHEET 15: SYNOPSIS

Objective: To create the synopsis for your reality show.

1. Fill in the blanks as it pertains to your reality show. The elements for a synopsis include: title of the show; number of episodes; genre; creator; subject ; what makes the subject special; what the subject will be involved with; the production team; outcome; and reason for the show.

Synopsis Template

_____, _____ of episodes, a _____ style reality show created
(Title of Show)   (#)   (Genre)

By _____ that follows _____. _____ is
   (Creator)   (Subject)   (Subject)

_____ and _____ as he/she or they do _____
(Attribute)   (Attribute)   (What the subject does)
_____.
(What the subject does)

_____ will be produced by _____, and directed
(Title of Show)   (Name of Company)

by _____. Join _____ as the _____
   (Director's Name)   (Subject)   (Outcome)

is achieved. _____.
             (Sentence to bring in Title of Show in a creative manner.)

2. Repeat above activity until you develop a synopsis the hones into your reality show.

3. Print a hardcopy of both the logline and synopsis and put in your binder.

NOTES

CHAPTER 6 WORKSHEETS

REALITY SHOW FORMAT

Photo by Razvan Ionut

WORKSHEET 16: BLUEPRINT

Objective 1: To identify blueprints to other reality shows.

Objective 2: Develop your blueprint for your reality show.

Title of Show

Genre: _____ ___ Episodes

Target Audience:

Beginning
How will your show open?

The Challenge:

Middle
Working on Challenge:

The Obstacle:

Almost reaching obstacle:

End
Overcoming Obstacle:

Reconciliation:

Closure:

2. Develop each of your episode breakdowns for your reality show.

Episode 1

Episode 2

Episode 3

Episode 4

Episode 5

Episode 6

Episode 7

Episode 8

Episode 9

Episode 10

Episode 11

Episode 12

Episode 13

Write down your reflection on this activity. How will it guide you to further develop your reality show?

NOTES

CHAPTER 7 WORKSHEETS

CAST

Photo by Salvatore Vuono

WORKSHEET 17: YOUR CAST

Objective: Generate a list of potential cast members for your project that follows their name, what they do, attributes, experience and whether they are attached to the project.

1. List the cast members you have already attached to your show.

   1. _____
   2. _____
   3. _____
   4. _____
   5. _____
   6. _____

2. List three potential cast members below that you think would be perfect for your show that could be possible substitutes.

   1. _____
   2. _____
   3. _____

3. Review your list above. Is there a variance in age, sex and ethnicity? If not, you might want to revisit the list. The more range the more likely there will be more appeal to potential audiences.

CAST   Page | 35

WORKSEET 18: CAST INFORMATION

Objective: To identify key attributes of each cast member.

Make enough copies of this worksheet that correlates to the number of your cast members.

Cast Member

Name: _____

Nickname: _____

Age: _____   M/F: _____

Ethnicity: _____   Profession: _____

What makes this person interesting?

What skill does this person have that makes them a good choice for your show?

What about this person that makes them interesting?

What experience do they bring to your project?

Is this person attached to the project?

WORKSHEET 19: CAST BIOS

Objective: Generate cast member's biographies for inclusion into your reality show plan.

1. Use the following template to generate your cast biographies.

The below bio statement includes all of the five elements and can serve as a guide post for describing each of your cast.

1. The cast member
2. Indicates what that cast member does.
3. Identifies key attributes about the cast member
4. Highlights her experience.
5. Details whether or not the cast member is attached to the project.

(1) "Rockyn" – Robbyn Stroud (2) is the Customer Service Specialist with a smile at Odom's Automotive. (3) She's full of laughter and absolutely loves people. Having worked as an inspector during major disasters she finds this job a little more upbeat. During her spare time she loves being with her kids and online dating. She knows the right man is out there, she just believes he lives on another planet – maybe Mars. (4) She has film experience as an extra on more than a dozen films. (3) Her Zodiac sign is Pieces. (5) "Rockyn" is attached to this project.

CAST MEMBER: _____

_____ is a _____ at _____.
(Name of Cast)   (Profession)   (Where they are employed)

He/She is known for _____, _____, and _____.
                    (List attribute) (List attribute) (List attribute)

He/She also believes _____.
(list something they believe are does in their spare time)

He/She has ____ experience in _____. _____ is/is not
   (# yrs if Experience)   (in film and/or television) (Name of Cast Member)

attached to this project.

CAST

Page | 37

CAST MEMBER: _____

_____ is a _____ at _____.
(Name of Cast)   *(Profession)*   *(Where they are employed)*

He/She is known for _____,_____, and _____.
                             (List attribute) (List attribute) (List attribute)

He/She also believes _____.
(list something they believe are does in their spare time)

He/She has _____ experience in _____. _____ is/is not
   (# yrs if Experience)   *(in film and/or television)*   *(Name of Cast Member)*

attached to this project.

CAST MEMBER: _____

_____ is a _____ at _____.
(Name of Cast)   *(Profession)*   *(Where they are employed)*

He/She is known for _____,_____, and _____.
                             (List attribute) (List attribute) (List attribute)

He/She also believes _____.
(list something they believe are does in their spare time)

He/She has _____ experience in _____. _____ is/is not
   (# yrs if Experience)   *(in film and/or television)*   *(Name of Cast Member)*

attached to this project.

NOTES

CHAPTER 8 WORKSHEETS

PRODUCTION TEAM

Photo by Salvatore Vuono

WORKSHEET 20: COMPANY STATEMENT

Objective: To formulate The Production Team opening statement.

1. Using the four import elements: company name, type of company, participants, and why the company was formed complete your opening statement.

Key:
1. Name of the company
2. Type of company formed
2. Participants in the company
4. Why the company was formed.

    The Company

    (1) Baker Girls, LLC, (2) a Limited Liability Company, (3) is an independent reality show production company that comprises experienced production professionals coupled with creative business (4) professionals with the common goal of producing the reality show, *The Baker Girls: Sealed with a Kiss.*

1. Answer the following questions.

1. What is the name of your company?

2. What type of company have you formed?

3. What individuals formed this company?

4. Why was the company formed?

2. Using your answers from above, formulate your opening statement.

3. Transfer your opening statement to your reality show business document. Print a hardcopy and put into your binder.

WORKSHEET 21: PRODUCER'S BIO

Objective: To formulate the producer's bio for your reality show business plan.

Answer the following questions.

1. Who is your producer?

2. What has your producer ever produced?

3. What business skills does the producer bring to your project?

4. What experience in production does your producer have?

5. What experience, other than production, makes this producer uniquely qualified?

6. Using the information above, generate a paragraph for your producer. Print a hardcopy and put into your binder.

WORKSHEET 22: DIRECTOR'S BIO

Objective: To formulate the director's bio for your reality show business plan.

Answer the following questions.

1. Who is your director?

2. What has your director directed or produced any reality shows, television or films?

3. What business skills does the director bring to your project?

4. What experience in production does your director have?

5. What experience, other than directing, makes this director uniquely qualified?

6. Is your director attached to the project?

7. Using the information above, generate a paragraph for your producer. Print a hardcopy and put into your binder.

WORKSHEET 23: CONSULTANTS

Objective: To identify affiliations and consultants.

1. Make a list of the people in the following table that you know and can rely on that will make your job as a creator and/or producer of a reality show easier.

Name of Contact	Area of Expertise	Contact Information

2. From the list above, contact each person and see if they are willing to be listed as a resource. (You cannot include them in your business plan unless they agree to do so.)

3. Make a list of business associations in the following table that you can refer to that will make your job as a creator and/or producer of a reality show.

Name of Business/Organization	Area of Expertise	Contact Information

4. Circle the contacts of individuals and Organizations above that have agreed to be listed in your plan. Print a hardcopy of each area and add to your binder.

CHAPTER 9 WORKSHEETS
PRODUCTION

Photo by Salvatore Vuono

WORKSHEET 24 : PRODUCTION SECTION

Objective: Write the Production section of your reality show business plan.

1. Are you developing a sizzle reel or a production outline for one or more episodes? Check the appropriate box.

   ☐ Sizzle Reel   ☐ 1 Pilot Episode   ☐ 4 – 7 Episodes   ☐ 8 -13 Episode

2. How many weeks do you think it will take for pre-production. Check the appropriate box.

   ☐ 1 Day   ☐ 3 Days   ☐ 6 Days

   ☐ 2 Weeks   ☐ 4-6 Weeks   ☐ More than 6 Weeks

Why do you think it will take this long?

3. How many days of shooting will it take to complete each episode?

   ☐ 1 Day   ☐ 3 Days   ☐ 5 Days   ☐ Other

4. How long will it take for the complete principal photography? _____ Weeks

5. How long do you think post-production or editing will take? _____ Weeks

6. Using the information above complete the "Production" section following the following format:

   > *There are three stages to producing a reality show: pre-production, production and post-production. During the pre-production stage all decisions regarding the production itself will be identified, cast members will be secured, crew will be attached, all locations for shooting will be identified, vendors will be located and contracted with and product placement will be considered. Pre-production **will take** ____ **weeks**. Once pre-production is completed, The Company will move into the production phase or principal photography **for** ____ **reality** show. During this **time** ___ **episodes** will be filmed. One each week until the story is completely developed. Principal photography will **last** ___ **weeks**. The Company upon completion of principal photography will immediately transition into post-production. All titling, music and sound will be inserted as well as clearly defined episodes that meet the story development arc. While in post-production, The Company will seek a distributor for the project. Post-production will **last** ____ **weeks**.*

7. Type the above statement into your reality show business plan.

CHAPTER 10 WORKSHEETS

REALITY SHOW STATISTICS

Photo by Carlos Portos

WORKSHEET 25: MARKET TREND

Objective: To identify the Reality Show Market Trend as it relates to your reality show project.

1. Answer the following questions?

List three similar reality shows currently airing on television?

How is your show the like the above shows?

How is show your different?

What show would your show most likely be competing against?

What television networks currently air your type of show?

What advertisers come on board?

2. Formulate your marketing paragraph for your business plan from the information you identified from above.

3. Place the paragraph into the appropriate section of your business plan. Print a hardcopy and place into your binder.

WORKSHEET 26: INDUSTRY TREND

Objective: To write a paragraph on current reality show Industry Trend for placement in your reality show business plan.

1. For the next seven days research and identify the ratings for current reality shows.

Show Title	Network	Rating

2. What type of reality show seems to be the most popular? Why do you think so?

3. Conduct an internet search and identify any new reality shows that are being picked up? Is there a trend? Look for network similarity, genres, producers etc.

4. Search on the internet the following bouillon key words:

Reality Show and Trends

Reality Top 10 Shows

Highest Rated Reality Show

Longest Running Reality Show

Reality Shows and Target Audiences

Networks and Reality Shows

Highest Gross and Reality Show

Networks Buying Reality Shows

Production Companies and Reality Shows

5. What key elements did you discover?

6. Find any facts and figures on how much reality shows have brought in during the last five years from a variety of sources online and in magazines.

7. Write a paragraph on the current trend for reality shows and include it in the proper section for your reality show business plan. Print a hardcopy and place into your binder.

CHAPTER 11 WORKSHEETS

PRODUCT-PLACEMENT

Photo by Renjith Krishnan

WORKSHEET 27: PRODUCT-PLACEMENT ITEMS

Objective: To identify future products for product-placement into your reality show.

1. Generate 15 products that either your current cast uses in everyday life.

1. _____   2. _____   3. _____

4. _____   5. _____   6. _____

1. _____   2. _____   3. _____

7. _____   8. _____   9. _____

10. _____ 11. _____ 12. _____

13. _____ 14. _____ 15. _____

2. Are there any specialty items that a specific cast member is known for? If so list cast member and item.

3. Does any cast member currently have a commercial or endorse products?

4. If the cast is being filmed at a work environment, list products that are natural to the environment?

5. What national company's product would lend itself for possible product-placement?

6. **In the appropriate section of your reality show business plan, outline the product-placement products following the format below or one you created.**

>Increasing revenue for advertisers should always be a goal for a reality show and (NAME OF YOUR SHOW) is perfect for product-placement. Throughout the show, each cast member uses (LIST A COMMON PRODUCT). What better way to highlight (NAME A PRODUCT) than by naturally using it and having (NAME A CAST MEMBER) comment on why HE/SHE insists on using (NAME AN ITEM) to (HOW IT IS USED). Also, what better way than for cast members to speak of the quality of (NAME A PRODUCT) and (NAME ANOTHER PRODUCT). This isn't a through it your face advertisement but rather a natural progression of how and why (NAME A PRODUCT) is used. The (NAME OF REALITY SHOW) holds unlimited potential for product placement to increase advertising revenue.

7. **Add completed product-placement statement into your reality show plan. Print a hardcopy and put into your binder.**

WORKSHEET 28: PRODUCT-PLACEMENT TABLE

Objective: To generate a Table that can be placed in your reality show business plan.

1. Identify 10 categories of products and potential companies for each category that your cast will naturally use; e.g., food, hair products, car products, clothing line, sunglasses, cell phones.

Product-Placement Category: _____	Product-Placement Category: _____
Product-Placement Category: _____	Product-Placement Category: _____
Product-Placement Category: _____	Product-Placement Category: _____
Product-Placement Category: _____	Product-Placement Category: _____
Product-Placement Category: _____	Product-Placement Category: _____
Product-Placement Category: _____	Product-Placement Category: _____

CHAPTER 12 WORKSHEETS

DISTRIBUTION

Photo by Renjith Krishnan

WORKSHEET 29: PRESS RELEASES

Objective: To write effective Press Releases.

1. Using the 5 Ws of who, what, when, where and why write and effective press release based off of the following information.

Who - Your Own Reality Show, LLC has joined with On the Lot Productions to produce your reality show.

What – The two companies will be producing the reality show, Making My Reality starring an up and coming first time creator and producer, which is you.

Where - You will be filming this show in your home town.

Why - You will be doing this show to enhance the careers of both production companies and show others the opportunity of creating shows.

When - Shooting is set to begin in three months.

Call to Action - You want people to come down and join the cast and be considered

2. Answer the following questions to generate your press release information.

1. Who is this press release about?

2. What is this press release about?

3. When will the event be happening?

4. Where will the even take place?

5. Why are you doing this?

3. Write your completed Press Release below.

4. Repeat this worksheet until you are comfortable writing press releases.

CHAPTER 13 WORKSHEETS

MARKETING STRATEGY

Photo by Renjith Krishnan

WORKSHEET 30: MARKETING STRATEGIES

Objective: To identify marketing strategies that can be incorporated into your reality show business plan.

1. Check the following market strategies that you could use in your reality business plan.

☐ Viral Marketing ☐ E-Mail Signature ☐ Website ☐ Blog cast ☐ Podcast

☐ Newsletter

☐ Youtube ☐ Vimeo ☐ Contests ☐ Give-a-ways ☐ Press Releases

2. Generate 15 other marketing strategy ideas.

1. _____ 2. _____ 3. _____
4. _____ 5. _____ 6. _____
1. _____ 2. _____ 3. _____
7. _____ 8. _____ 9. _____
10. _____ 11. _____ 12. _____
13. _____ 14. _____ 15. _____

3. Ask at least 3 friends for their marketing strategy ideas. Include them in the space below if they are not already checked or listed above.

4. Following the suggested format develop your opening statement for your Marketing Strategy section. Print a hardcopy and place into your binder.

WORKSHEET 31: MARKETING STATEMENT

Objective: To identify marketing strategies that can be incorporated into your reality show business plan.

Use the following format to create your Marketing Strategy Statement for your business plan.

1. Name of company

2. Varied marketing techniques

3. Name of show.

> (1) The key to a successful reality show is proportionately related to The Company's marketing campaign and strategy. (2) Hoops, LLC will incorporate sound marketing strategies to promote the reality show (3) *Hoops: Life off the Court*.
>
> **"Marketing Strategy"**

CHAPTER 14 WORKSHEETS

INVESTMENT OPPORTUNITY.

Photo by Pixomar

Note: There are no worksheets for Chapter 14 that goes with my book, The Reality of Reality TV: Reality Show Business Plans. The topic is addressed completely in the book.

CHAPTER 15 WORKSHEETS
THE ONE PAGER

Graphics and Photo designed by On the Lot Productions, LLC, Copyright ©2011

WORKSHEET 32: THE ONE PAGER

Objective: To develop the One Pager for inclusion into your reality show business plan.

1. Using the format below develop your One Pager.

PLACE LOGO GRAPHICS OF SHOW HERE

Genre: _____ Reality Show
Length: _____ Minutes
_____ Episodes
_____ Format

LOGLINE:

SYNOPSIS:

TARGET AUDIENCE:

Name of Production Company
Contact Information

---

2. Put together a different One Pager with a different font and use a jpeg image for your graphics along with the title of your show. Determine which one you like the best.

THE ONE PAGER   Page | 67

Place JPEG Image

TITLE OF YOUR REALITY SHOW HERE

Genre: _____ Reality Show
Length: _____ Minutes
_____ Episodes
_____ Format

LOGLINE:

SYNOPSIS:

TARGET AUDIENCE:

Name of Production Company
Contact Information

NOTES

CHAPTER 16 WORKSHEETS

THE BUDGET

Photo by Pixomar

WORKSHEET 33: LINE ITEMS

Objective: Identify Line items as it relates to your project.

1. Using the following line items circle the ones that you will need to include for your production of your sizzle reel and/or pilot reality show.

Above the Line Categories
1100   Story rights and Continuity
1200   Producer's Unit
1300   Director's Unit
1400   Cast
1500   Cast Travel and Lodging
1900   Cast Fringe Benefits and Taxes

Below the Line Categories for Production
2000   Production Staff
2100   Extra Talent and Atmosphere
2200   Art Direction
2300   Set Construction and Strike
2400   Set Operations
2500   Special Effects
2600   Set Dressing
2700   Property
2800   Wardrobe
2900   (Left Open)
3000   (Left Open)
3100   Lighting Equipment
3200   Camera Equipment
3300   Grip Gear
3400   Production Sound
3500   Transportation
3600   Location
3700   Production of Film & Lab
3800   Still Photography

3900   Test Shoots
4000   2nd Unit
4100   Production Office
4200   Production Office Supplies
4300   Production Fringe Benefits and Taxes
4400   (Left Open)

Below the Line Cost for Post Production
4500   Editing
4600   Music
4700   Post Production Sound
4800   Post Production Film & Lab
4900   Main & End Titles
5000   (Left Open)
5100   (Left Open)
5200   Post Production Fringe Benefits and Taxes

Other Below the Line Cost
6500   Publicity & Promotion
6600   Website and Graphics
6700   Insurance
6800   Overhead
6900   Miscellaneous
7000   Finance Fee
7100   Completion Bond
7200   Contingency

THE BUDGET

2. How many days of production are you planning?

3. How many locations will you need and what are the cost per day for their usage?

4. What equipment do you currently have on hand that you would not need to purchase or rent?

5. Using the formula below calculate your approximate cost for each line item.

Line Item is:

Number of days X number of cast/crew/equipment = Line item Cost

WORKSHEET 34: POTENTIAL CREW

Objective: To identify potential crew and vendors for the production of your reality show sizzle reel and/or pilot episode.

Answer the following questions.

1. Make a list of people you know that own film equipment.

Name: _____

Equipment: _____

Name: _____

Equipment: _____

Name: _____

Equipment: _____

Name: _____

Equipment: _____

Name: _____

Equipment: _____

Name: _____

Equipment: _____

Name: _____

Equipment: _____

THE BUDGET

WORKSHEET 35: POTENTIAL VENDORS

1. Identify vendors in your computer that rent production equipment.

Name: _____

Equipment: _____

Name: _____

Equipment: _____

Name: _____

Name: _____

Equipment: _____

Name: _____

Equipment: _____

Name: _____

Equipment: _____

Name: _____

Equipment: _____

Name: _____

Equipment: _____

WORKSHEET 36: POTENTIAL Locations

1. Make a list of business owners you know that may allow you to use their places as locations.

Name: _____

Location: _____

Name: _____

Location: _____

Name: _____

Name: _____

Location: _____

Name: _____

Location: _____

Name: _____

Name: _____

Location: _____

Name: _____

3. Contact everybody on your list above and see if they are interested in participating in your reality show.

THE BUDGET   Page | 75

WORKSHEET 37: BUDGET PROJECTION

1. Use the following table to generate your Summary Top Sheet. Use the circled line items categories circled from Worksheet 32 to generate your line items needed for your production. You will need to make enough copies in accordance with the number of line items as well as for above-the-line and below the line costs.

Example:

Line Item No	Description	Cost	X	Number of Days	=	Total of Line Item
1200	Producer	1000	X	4 Days	=	1000
3200	Camera Equipment	375	X	2 Days	=	750

List the Line Items that you need for your production.

BUDGET TOP SUMMARY SHEET

Line Item No	Description	Cost	X	Number of Days	=	Total Amount of Line Item
			X		=	
			X		=	
			X		=	
			X		=	
			X		=	
			X		=	
			X		=	
			X		=	
			X		=	
			X		=	
			X		=	
			X		=	
			X		=	
			X		=	
			X		=	
			X		=	
			X		=	
			X		=	
			X		=	
			X		=	
			X		=	
			X		=	
			X		=	
			X		=	
			X		=	
			X		=	
			X		=	
			X		=	
			X		=	

TOTAL OF LINE ITEMS: _____

CHAPTER 17 WORKSHEETS

PUTTING IT ALL TOGETHER

Graphics Designed by On the Lot Productions, LLC © Copyright 2011
Photo by Simon Howden

WORKSHEET 38: EDITING AND FORMATTING

Objective: To review your reality show business plan to make certain that all criteria have been adhered to.

Review your business plan document adhering to the following benchmarks. Check off completed tasks.

- ☐ I have re-visited my Executive Summary section and replaced on XXXs with appropriate data

- ☐ I have proof read my plan for spelling and grammar errors

- ☐ I have added pictures and graphics to the document that enhances the overall presentation

- ☐ I have established the Appendix section

- ☐ All headings and subheadings are consistent in format

- ☐ My Table of Contents have been created and page numbers reflected

- ☐ Other people have proof read my business plan

- ☐ I have printed and filed away a hard copy of my final plan

- ☐ I have saved several copies of my business plan on numerous jump drives.

- ☐ I have E-Mailed a copy to my own E-Mail address

- ☐ I have registered my business plan Document with WGA

- ☐ I have put my WGA number on the cover sheet of my business plan.

WORKSHEET 39: PARTS OF THE BUSINESS PLAN

Objective: To identify and complete all parts of a reality show business plan.

Check all parts that have been completed in your reality show business plan.

- ☐ The Cover
- ☐ The Confidentiality Agreement
- ☐ Table of Contents
- ☐ The Executive Summary
- ☐ The Logline and Synopsis
- ☐ The Structure of the Show
- ☐ The Cast Members
- ☐ The Production Team
- ☐ Production and Production Schedule
- ☐ The Market
- ☐ Product Placement
- ☐ Distribution
- ☐ Marketing Strategy
- ☐ Investment Opportunity
- ☐ The One-Pager
- ☐ The Budget
- ☐ The Appendix Cover Sheet
- ☐ Resumes
- ☐ Letters of intent for:
- ☐ Producer ☐ Production Company ☐ Director ☐ Cast
- ☐ News clippings

CHAPTER 18 WORKSHEETS

FIRST CONTACT

Photo by Simon Howden

NOTES

WORKSHEET 40: NETWORK CONTACTS

Objective: Make contact with television networks.

1. Mark the Television Network that your show would best fit into their existing line-up. Check all that apply.

☐ ABC   ☐ NBC   ☐ A & E   ☐ CBS   ☐ FOX   ☐ FX   ☐ PBS   ☐ CW   ☐ BET   ☐ BRAVO

☐ MTV   ☐ DISCOVERY   ☐ ESPN   ☐ OXYGEN   ☐ TLC   ☐ USA   ☐ VH1   ☐ OTHER: _____

2. Indentify production companies that would most likely be interested in your type of reality show.

Name of Company	Contact Information	Shows They Produced

3. Identify 10 Literary Agents.

NAME OF AGENT OR AGENCY	CONTACT INFORMATION

4. Begin contacting all television networks, production companies and agents listed above. Be sure to maintain a contact log so you can follow up.

5. Maintain a log of contacts and place a hardcopy in your binder.

WORKSHEET 41: THE AGENT QUERY LETTER

Objective: To construct a query letter for literary agent acquisition.

Query letters have three parts: hook, synopsis, bio information and end with your request.

1. Complete the following to write your query letter to obtain an agent.

THE HOOK: (Write logline in the space below)

THE SYNOPSIS: (Write the shortened version of the logline here)

BIO: (Write a smaller version of your bio here)

REQUEST: (Write your statement that you are seeking a literary agent)

2. Using word processing software format your query letter and have it ready to go. Print a hardcopy and place it into your binder.

WORKSHEET 42: NETWORK QUERY LETTER

Objective: To construct a query letter to send to a television network.

Query letters have three parts: hook, synopsis, bio information and end with your request.

1. Complete the following to write your query letter to a television network.

THE HOOK: (Write logline in the space below)

HOW YOUR SHOW FITS WITH THE NETWORK

THE SYNOPSIS: (Write the shortened version of the logline here)

BIO: (Write a smaller version of your bio here)

REQUEST: (Write your statement that you are seeking to green-light your project from a production company)

2. Using word processing software format your television query letter and have it ready to go. Print a hardcopy and place it into your binder.

WORKSHEET 43: PRODUCTION QUERY LETTER

Objective: To construct a query letter to send to a production company.

Query letters have three parts: hook, synopsis, bio information and end with your request.

1. Complete the following to write your query letter to a production company.

THE HOOK: (Write logline in the space below)

THE SYNOPSIS: (Write the shortened version of the logline here)

BIO: (Write a smaller version of your bio here)

REQUEST: (Write your statement that you are seeking to green-light your project from a production company)

2. Using word processing software format your production query letter and have it ready to go. Print a hardcopy and place into your binder.

CHAPTER 19

GOING FORWARD

Graphics created by On the Lot Productions, LLC © Copyright 2011

You have consistently been dedicated to completing the worksheets in this book and applying yourself. Congratulations. If you purchased my book, *The Reality of Reality TV: Reality Show Business Plans*, and applied yourself by now should have a completed a reality show business plan tailored specifically for your show. If you tried to take a shortcut and only purchased this workbook, I have no idea what your results are going are or for that matter if your plan makes any sense at all. I sincerely hope that you took my advice and bought the companion book. That is the only way to get excellent results. Remember, there are no second chances to make a first impression to Hollywood Insiders. Your goal should always present yourself and your show in a professional manner. The information in my companion book will do just that and it is a one of a kind book. There is nothing on the market like it. Trust me. I did my research.

Also in the companion book is a complete example of the business plan for my show *Hoops: Life of the Court* for your review. That fact alone I am told is the reason other creators and producers bought that book. They needed guidance and assistance.

A word of caution, please remember that business plans for reality shows are different from those for films. You won't get the results you need by following a business plan for a film. Also, remember there is no such thing as a boilerplate business plan. If anyone tries to tell you differently please don't fall for it. Every reality show business plan must be written specifically for each show. Therefore, don't take the lazy way out and copy my plan or plans from others. You will likely cause more harm than get green-light. Although I do have available a reality show business plan template, it is just that – a template and not boilerplate business plan.

By submitting your completed plan tailored for your show to the right television executive it could be the biggest change in your professional career. How to go about this task is also found in my companion book and will not be repeated here.

I hope the journey has been an amazing one and that you reap great rewards. I hope you have taken away new knowledge and a skill that you can use again in the near future and be successful. Don't stop at creating just one reality show but create as many as you can. One of them is bound to land on the desk of a Hollywood Insider. Good luck! Hope to see your project on television. Please let me know when it does by zapping me an email to drmelcaudle@gmail.com.

ABOUT THE AUTHOR

Dr. Melissa Caudle earned a Ph.D. in statistical research and administration from the University of New Orleans. She is a retired award winning high school principal who came into the television and film production arena in 1986. Capitalizing on her educational training and background, she uses her experience and training to bring the reader a resource and step-by-step guided teaching format to learn how to create reality show business plans and concepts.

Dr. Melissa Caudle is also an experienced reality show creator and producer and brings her expertise in the area of writing business plans for reality shows to you the reader. Dr. Mel has built a solid reputation as a reality show creator having started as a production coordinator in New Orleans, La on the reality show, *The Girls Next Door* featuring the three Playmates and Hugh Hefner. That was the beginning of transferring her knowledge from feature film production. She discovered quickly that although there were vast similarities there were also vast differences. Two huge differences were pitching a reality show and developing a business plan for one. Isolating the differences came by applying her experience as an adjunct professor, teacher and researcher. "I never knew that a Ph.D. in Statistical Analysis would prove beneficial in creating reality shows and business plans, "she says. "But it did."

Since that time Dr. Mel has created five reality shows, produced four, and is currently in the process of developing two others at the time she wrote this book. . Dr. Mel is the producer and director of the reality show featuring Darren Sharper, Super Bowl Champion with the New Orleans Saints, called *Darren: Sharper than Ever*, created and is currently producing the reality Show *The Ace Mechanic* , Hoops: *Life off the Court*, and *The Baker Girls: Sealed with a Kiss* all of which she wrote the business plans. Additionally she is the field producer for two other reality shows, *"Sixteen Weeks"* and *"What's Hot, What's Not"* currently in production in New Orleans, LA.

Producers and creators of reality shows consult with Dr. Mel on writing a business plan specifically for reality shows. She also develops reality show business plans as a part of her production company, On the Lot Productions, LLC located in New Orleans, LA. She is part of The Alliance Film Team.

"It's a tangled web that nobody wants to share how to develop," she says. "That is until now. I'm taking my 12 years of experience in production and tapping into my experience as a teacher and professor to bring knowledge to those who seek."

Dr. Mel is also a feature and documentary filmmaker. Her credits include producer on the feature film *Dark Blue* and associate producer on the films *Varla Jean and the Mushroomheads* and *Girls Gone Gangsta*. *She* also produced and directed documentary films including *Mexico Missions, The Dolphins in Terry Cove, The Alabama Gulf Coast Zoo, Sean Kelly's Irish Pub, Beauvoir* and *Voices of the Innocent*.

Dr. Mel has worked as a crew member on films such as the two Sony films, *STRAWDOGS* starring Kate Bosworth, James Marsden, and Alexander Skarsgard, and *MARDI GRAS* starring Carmen Electra and television programs such as the television reality series *GIRLS NEXT DOOR* as production coordinator and *THE LITTLE COUPLE*. She also has been a program director for a television station in Alabama. Her company, On the Lot Productions, LLC is currently in pre-production on another independent film. Dr. Mel has written eight screenplays: *Auditing Richard Biggs*, *A.D.A.M.*, *MK*-ULTRA, *The Angelics* (Sci-fi); *Dreamweaver* (Drama), *Dragonfly Principal* (Drama), *Never Stop Running* (Suspense/Thriller) and *Secret* Romance (Romantic Comedy). She has placed in the Scriptdig Screenplay Contest as a Quarter-finalist in both screenplay and TV pilot category and was a semi-finalist in The Page International Screenwriting Contest.

  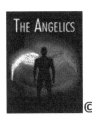  

A.D.A.M written by Dr. Melissa Caudle
MK-Ultra written by Dr. Melissa Caudle
Auditing Richard Biggs written by Dr. Melissa Caudle and Dennis W. Martin
Secret Romance written by Dr. Melissa Caudle
Never Stop Running written by Dr. Melissa Caudle
The Angelics written by Dr. Melissa Caudle and David Repogle
Dreamweaver written by Dr. Melissa Caudle and Michael Ragsdale
Dragonfly Principal written by Dr. Melissa Caudle and Gabriel Dyan

Reality Shows

ABOUT THE AUTHOR

For more information on the books, screenplays or reality shows by Dr. Mel Caudle visit her website located at: www.drmelcaudle.com or www.onthelorproductions.com. To contact Dr. Mel for a speaking engagement email her at drmelcaudle@google.com.

B

Big 5 "W's", 8
biographies, 36
blueprints, 30
BUDGET TOP SUMMARY SHEET, 76
business plan, 1, 2, 33

C

cast, 19
concept, 7
Confidentiality, 5, 14, 79
consultants, 43
crew, 9, 46, 71, 72, 90

D

director's bio, 42
distribution, 22

E

episode breakdowns, 31
Executive Summary, 16, 17, 20, 22, 78, 79

G

graphics, 11

I

Industry Trend, 49
Investment Opportunity, 23

K

key attributes, 35

L

Line items, 70
locations, 74
logline, 11, 26, 27, 84, 85, 86

M

Market Trend, 48
marketing strategies, 3, 22, 60, 61
Marketing Trend Statement, 18

O

On the Lot Productions production company, 2
One Pager, 6, 66
Opening Statement, 16
Overview Statement, 17

P

Press Releases, 6, 56, 60
producer's bio, 41

Q

query letter, 84, 85, 86

R

reality show business plan, 1, 2
reality show genres
documentary,game show,life drama,dating shows,special environment,celebrity,competition,surveillance, talk shows, professional ativities, 6

S

synopsis, 11, 27, 84, 85, 86

T

Template, 2
title, 10

V

vendors, 21, 46, 72, 73

Production section, 46
Production Team, 5, 20, 40, 79
Production Team Statement, 20
product-placement, 21, 52, 53

Made in the USA
Lexington, KY
10 April 2015